By. Jill H. Remington

5 Easy Steps To Sell Your Home!

INTRODUCTION

Welcome to my new E-series, **"HOW TO BE HIGHLY PROFITABLE AND EFFECTIVE IN YOUR REAL ESTATE DEALINGS."** In this E-series, you will get some of my top insights, strategies, and experiences gained during my highly prestigious and professional real estate career as a Global Real Estate Advisor & Broker. From Philadelphia to Beverly Hills, from Hong Kong, Singapore, Manilla to London, they have proven to work consistently and geographically. As a Seller or a Buyer, the proven strategies laid out before you will assist you in becoming highly effective and more profitable. The initial concept was to write an E-series of real estate books that took only about five minutes to read, five hours to contemplate, and about five days to fully implement. Like it or not, we are in the texting generation where sound bites might only be 3 minutes long so it's very important to get it right. You might say, "I want it, I want it now, and I want it delivered!" With this in mind, my E-series was born. I have included several insider Pro Tips to emphasize the importance of each subject matter.

Chapter I

Step 1 PUT YOUR MONEY WHERE IT SHOWS!

PRIORITIZE YOUR EXPENDITURES

I learned a long time ago in this business that the most important thing you can do is my first Pro Tip.

PRO TIP: PUT YOUR MONEY WHERE IT SHOWS!

Hands Down! When you show your home to prospective buyers, first impressions are made usually made within 3-5 minutes. You only have one shot at their first impressions. Needless to say, these first impressions are critical to you as a seller and critical to them as buyers. It is at this stage where the buyers are deciding if they want to proceed. That is why it is so important to research before placing your home on the market. Buyers come with a purpose-driven mission. Do I buy or not? The good news is that they want to purchase a home. They will enter your home with eyes like an eagle. I have coined a term over the years for them. I call them "BWR'", an acronym for Buyers with Radar. They are visually scanning your home for important issues to them. Like, are there any value-added items such as updated lighting fixtures? What is the current overall condition and age of your home? Are the cabinets, kitchen appliances, countertops, flooring, and other eye-catching features something we like, could live with, or have to replace? For this reason, I say, don't waste your time or money on things that don't show when you can put that money into things that do. Save the unseen or barely noticed for the home inspection period.

Start by setting a pre-sale budget to freshen up or update your property. Then prioritize your budget. Do the most important things the buyers will see first. A good way to determine what type of value you can add to attract buyers is to do a real estate search for comparable properties in your area. Which one's sold and which one's didn't? Review the photos of both, sold and unsold and then you will see where they put their money or which features made one property sell over the other. Again, know where to put your money.

If you want the biggest bang for your buck - take a lead from home flippers. Change out your older lighting fixtures for modern new ones. Everyone likes new. Nothing makes a bigger impact in updating or staging your home than new current lighting. Flippers do it automatically because this is where your eyes are drawn and sets the tone for first impressions. Ask yourself, what is the trending style right now? Be sure and double-check that the style you like is not on the way out. The farmhouse was very popular over the last few years, followed by Mid-Century Modern. but both are fading and I'm seeing a large influx of Industrial Style mixed with more sustainable wovens such as wicker and rattan. You want your investment to count and add to your bottom line so choose wisely. Always consider scale. Too small look cheap and can give an appearance of off balance. Too big and it can be overwhelming. A lighting pro, usually a free service, at any lamp store can help you with scale. Take in the measurements and a picture of where the lighting fixture will go. If you are purchasing online in stores such as Wayfair, Houzz , Elm Street, and others, measure it out yourself in your space before you buy. There are many beautiful styles to select from so choose for your bottom line and don't break the bank. Forward-thinking for a style choice is key.

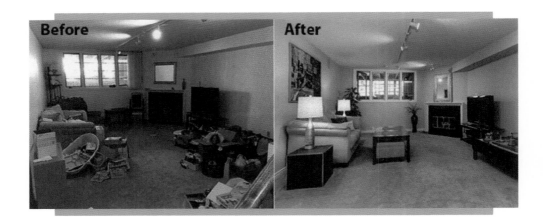

Before **After**

Putting your money where it shows includes getting rid of all the clutter. Clutter is bad, it is distracting and will be an unwanted distraction to your buyers. The most basic task when staging a home is to remove all the clutter and deep clean your house. It is also a good idea to remove knick-knacks and personal items from all your surfaces. In this case, less is better. Store your items in boxes in your garage Don't store the clutter in your closets. Potential buyers usually look in your closets and cabinets and you want yours to appear roomy. With all the clutter gone, it will be a lot easier to do a deep cleaning. Make sure your kitchen, bathrooms, and windows are sparkly clean. Let them see how nice the views to the outside are. This will make your home appear more spacious. Before a showing, air out the entire house by opening the windows, which is much better than air fresheners or scented candles. Candles can easily trigger allergies. I have had personal clients turn around and not walk through a property because the pet smell, cooking odors, or scented candles were too strong. Recently, in one of my million-dollar listings, my client had a scented candle burning. The buyers came through and asked if the home was older than it looked because it smelled very musty. I told her about it for future showings and her response was, "Well it came from Anthropology and it was expensive." Anthropology or not, if the buyers don't like it, you could protentional lose a sell. She stopped burning the candle and her home sold. Was it the smell? Maybe. If you don't want to clean yourself, consider hiring a pro for the deep clean. For staging help, you can also hire an interior designer to give you suggestions on how to better stage your home. I often have FaceTime calls with my clients in real estate where they will walk me through their homes. We take one room at a time or they send me photographs. I will do a quick Design Review for them and this has been very successful. There are also construction companies that will do your home improvement or repairs for your presale and bill you directly through your escrow. These simple steps will go a long way to make your home look more marketable and put more money in your pocket at the end of the day.

Chapter 2

Step2 TAKE AMAZING PHOTOGRAPHS!

The next step can't be overrated.

PRO TIP: SHOOT TO SELL!

Pictures are worth a thousand words and they do count. Look at the before and after shots, I have included. The picture quality can make a difference in how long the buyer will look at your photographs. After all, who wants to go preview a dark room? My point, would you rather drink out of a glass that had a residue film on it, or a crystal clear one? Resolution is key!

PRO TIP: ONLY USE HIGH-RESOLUTION PICS!

Get amazing photographs of your home's interior and exterior with a wide-angle lens. If you have a good eye and a good camera, most smartphones do have good cameras, then you can take the photographs yourself. The next big step is to prove all photographs before you use them. Look for things that the camera captured but you were not aware of it until you proofed the photograph. Maybe a toy, shovel, pool towel, etc. from outside that you can see through the window.

Maybe something left on the floor, an item on the counter, or anything that stands out that you don't want in your picture. Cameras never lie so make sure it's the shot you wanted. Exterior unwanted shots could include ugly powerlines, neighbors' unsightly yards, trash cans exposed, etc. So, proof every picture and recapture the shot if necessary, from a different angle. Make sure your home is staged without clutter and lighted properly for all your photographs.

PRO TIP: USE CREATIVE ANGLES WITH CORRECT LIGHTING!

Creative angles from your POV will create the most interesting perspectives. My minor in college was photography and I learned how effective and profitable angle shots can be. They are more artistic, interesting, and give a different perspective. It is like having art on a camera. Cinematographers win Oscars for their creative POV angles. Get creative and it will pay off. High-resolution Photographs with proper lighting will set the stage to showcase your home at its best in Step # 5 below.

Chapter 3

Step3 SPREAD THE WORD!

SPREAD THE WORD!

PRO TIP:	MARKETING FOR SALE BY OWNER

The next part is going to require work on your part, but it can be a lot of fun once you understand how the different social media platforms work. You can use a few, most, or all of them for maximum value. Here are a few standard ones to get you started. Facebook, Instagram, Twitter, FSBO, Google. You can google them and then select the ones you want. It will give you a huge advantage over other sellers to have your presence online and combine it with a specified schedule. The more social media hubs you connect with, the greater the exposure, maximizing your home's value. You might be surprised to see who is interested in your home. From friends, family, and colleagues, leave no stone unturned for they can assist you in spreading the word and you could end up in a sale. Yahoo!

Chapter 4

Step4 Put up a large FOR Sale Sign!

Place a large for sale sign up in your front yard that creates the most visible presence. If you live in a condominium, townhouse, or multi-dwellings you may be able to place it in a window that has the most exposure from the street. Please check with your local HOA first for any sign ordinances before investing any money into a sign. Your sign is your flag. Wave it proudly!

PRO TIP: ADD CONTACT INFORMATION!

Make sure your sign includes a contact name, phone number and can be read or photographed from a car. PRO TIP: CREATE A QR CODE! I would also recommend going online and creating a specific QR Code with your contact information. You can also purchase stickers that can be placed on your sign. I included mine as an example.

Go ahead and scan it. It works. Creating one for your home will work for you too. Buyers love it. It's simple, noninvasive, and gets them more information instantly. Another step and reason to contact you.

Chapter 5

Step5 START YOUR SOCIAL MEDIA CAMPAIGN!

With the current Covid Culture, Social Media is 100% your BFF right now.

PRO TIP: GO ALL IN!

Select your favorite Social Media Platforms and start a campaign. A word of caution, however, establish first that the platform doesn't share the listings with any other websites, the agreement is between you and the partner. This disclosure is to help to prevent any fraud and/or liability on your part. Request traffic and analytics be sent to you on a daily or weekly basis. This is your campaign report card. According to a recent 2021 real estate survey, 80% of all home sales begin on the internet.

PRO TIP: : USE CAMPAIGN TECH TOOLS!

Use valuable tech tools such as virtual walkthroughs, artificial intelligence, and augmented reality to boost your position in the marketplace. This is a famous retail business saying, "80% of all sales are made on the approach level." If that is true, then social media would be the runway! I would also recommend you supplement your campaign with an effective print campaign. Create and print out beautiful colored brochures to hand out to your potential buyers when they preview your home.

I would also highly recommend you start by making a YouTube campaign video. This is state-of-the-art advertising and one of the most effective campaign tools you can use. You can visit my video channel at YouTube.com/jillremington and see real examples of how effective and beautiful campaigns can be. You can create it yourself, hire a videographer or for less money hire a wedding photographer to help you.

I hope you enjoyed and benefited from my new E-Series on "How To Best Sell Your Home Highly & Effectively." To be automatically updated on this information and receive new information, please sign on to my website subscription service. You can reach it by scanning the QR Code above. It's free. If you have any questions, you can submit them in the comment section of my blog birchstreet. blog and I will do my best to answers them in my future E-Series publications. Thank you and much success in "Selling Your Home Highly & Effectively!"

Happy selling.

About the Author Jill H. Remington

With over 25 years of owning and operating several independent real estate brokerages and luxury design firms throughout California and Arizona, plus more than $325 million in career sales and real estate developments, it's no wonder author and award-winning Global Real Estate Advisor and Broker Jill H. Remington gets high praises not just from clients, but also from CBS, Good Morning Arizona, CNNfn, and NYC.

Having been a Managing General Partner at JARIC Developers in Los Angeles, Jill helped successfully build over three million square feet of office, R&D, and commercial–industrial spaces throughout Southern California.

As a seasoned Global Real Estate Advisor and Broker, Jill works with several major national Joint Venture Partners, including Ahmanson Commercial Development, Teacher's Insurance & Annuity, NYC, Citi Corporation, and many others in Singapore, Hong Kong, Manila, London, and Canada.

Her current focus is on enhancing the consumer experience and elevating the status of the residential brokerage profession by encouraging innovation, transparency, ethics, advocacy, influence, best practices, and education.

Today, Jill distills all her experiences, hard-earned truths, and industry savvy in comprehensive, practical, easy-to-follow guides that get readers tangible results, including her most awaited eBook series "How to Be Highly Profitable and Effective in Your Real Estate Dealings."

All of her success is built on strong work ethics and passion. Jill attended the University of California at Santa Barbara, holds two United States Design Patents, and has been featured in two bestselling books — Faces of Arizona and Angels of Arizona.

When she's not writing or selling and developing property, Jill spends her time as a Patron of the American Red Cross, Pediatrics for Children, and St. Jude's Foundation. She also enjoys spending time with her family in their wonderful Scottsdale, Arizona home.

For more information about Jill, her books, and her work, visit jillremington.com today.

THE FOLLOWING NOTEBOOK PAGES ARE ADDED FOR YOUR CONVIENCE
Here you can add important information such as contacts, vendors, bids, and scheduling.

THE FOLLOWING NOTEBOOK PAGES ARE ADDED FOR YOUR CONVIENCE
Here you can add important information such as contacts, vendors, bids, and scheduling.

THE FOLLOWING NOTEBOOK PAGES ARE ADDED FOR YOUR CONVIENCE
Here you can add important information such as contacts, vendors, bids, and scheduling.

THE FOLLOWING NOTEBOOK PAGES ARE ADDED FOR YOUR CONVIENCE
Here you can add important information such as contacts, vendors, bids, and scheduling.

THE FOLLOWING NOTEBOOK PAGES ARE ADDED FOR YOUR CONVIENCE
Here you can add important information such as contacts, vendors, bids, and scheduling.

THE FOLLOWING NOTEBOOK PAGES ARE ADDED FOR YOUR CONVIENCE
Here you can add important information such as contacts, vendors, bids, and scheduling.

THE FOLLOWING NOTEBOOK PAGES ARE ADDED FOR YOUR CONVIENCE
Here you can add important information such as contacts, vendors, bids, and scheduling.

THE FOLLOWING NOTEBOOK PAGES ARE ADDED FOR YOUR CONVIENCE
Here you can add important information such as contacts, vendors, bids, and scheduling.

THE FOLLOWING NOTEBOOK PAGES ARE ADDED FOR YOUR CONVIENCE
Here you can add important information such as contacts, vendors, bids, and scheduling.

THE FOLLOWING NOTEBOOK PAGES ARE ADDED FOR YOUR CONVIENCE
Here you can add important information such as contacts, vendors, bids, and scheduling.

THE FOLLOWING NOTEBOOK PAGES ARE ADDED FOR YOUR CONVIENCE
Here you can add important information such as contacts, vendors, bids, and scheduling.

THE FOLLOWING NOTEBOOK PAGES ARE ADDED FOR YOUR CONVIENCE
Here you can add important information such as contacts, vendors, bids, and scheduling.

Printed in Great Britain
by Amazon